Towards Transnational Parties in the European Community

Geoffrey Pridham and
Pippa Pridham

Studies in European Politics 2

Studies in European Politics

This series provides brief and up-to-date analyses of European political issues, including developments in the European Community and in transnational political forces, and also major problems in particular European countries. The research is undertaken by the European Centre for Political Studies, established in 1978 at the Policy Studies Institute with the sponsorship of the European Cultural Foundation. The series is edited by the Head of the Centre, Dr Roger Morgan.

Studies scheduled for publication in 1979 include:

1. The Future of the European Parliament   *David Coombes*
2. Towards Transnational Parties in the European Community   *Geoffrey & Pippa Pridham*
3. European Integration, Regional Devolution and National Parliaments   *D. Coombes, L. Condorelli, R. Hrbek, W. Parsons, S. Schüttemeyer*
4. Eurocommunism: the Foreign Policy Dimensions   *Carole Webb*
5. Liberalism in the European Community   *Ove Guldberg and Niels Haagerup*
6. Social Democracy in the European Community   *Norbert Gresch*
7. Political Forces in Spain, Greece and Portugal   *Beate Kohler*
8. Parliament and the Economy in Four West European Countries   *G. Amato, A. Dupas, J. Kooiman, S. Walkland*

Of related interest

Westminster and Devolution   *Study of Parliament Group in association with PSI*

ISBN 0 85374 170 0

Published by PSI, 1/2 Castle Lane, London SW1E 6DR
Printed by Dawson & Goodall Ltd., The Mendip Press, Bath

Contents

page

I   **What is Transnational Party Co-operation?**   1

II   **The Euro-Parliamentary Dimension**   4
The European Parliament   4
The political and administrative importance of the groups   5
Criteria applicable to this form of transnational activity   6
The possible impact of direct elections   9

III   **The Transnational Party Organisational Dimension**   11
The constitutional basis of the federations and their institutional interlinkage within the European Community   13
The envisaged electoral role of the federations and patterns of their political activity   15

IV   **The National Party Frameworks and Transnational Co-operation**   18
The party-traditional factor   19
The political-functional factor   22
The socio-political factor   24

I

What is Transnational Party Co-operation?

Transnational party co-operation in the European Community (EC) is the term applied to the harmonisation or co-ordination of European policy positions by political parties of the same ideological tendency from different member countries within a common institutional framework at the Community level. With a history that derives from the first efforts at such co-operation within the Common Assembly of the European Coal and Steel Community (ECSC) in the earlier 1950s, this form of activity has until recent times implied primarily, if not exclusively, the operation of party groups within the European Parliament. During the course of the present decade, and specifically from the mid-1970s, transnational party co-operation has both extended beyond its Euro-Parliamentary form and assumed a new organisational and political importance in response to conscious initiatives, the widening scope of European integration itself and, notably, the direct stimulus of prospective elections to the European Parliament. To what extent can one therefore begin to speak realistically of transnational political parties in the European Community?

As transnational party co-operation is in the process of further crystallisation, this development—which evidently amounts to the most important stage in the evolution of Community-level party activity since the informal initiation of European parliamentary groups nearly a generation ago—raises several wider questions.

Firstly, transnational party co-operation cannot be considered without reference to the general institutional context within which it takes place. This in turn points to the problem of what kind of enveloping 'political system' is constituted by the European Community. Here historical models are misleading, as concepts like the 'United States of Europe' have remained over time within the realm of aspirations rather than of practical possibility, while the current use of the word 'confederation' in national governmental circles is at best very loose encompassing several different interpretations. The safest

---

For a fuller discussion, see the authors' two chapters (11 and 12) in Stanley Henig (ed), *Political Parties in the European Community* (Allen and Unwin, 1979) and also their forthcoming book, *Transnational Party Co-operation and Direct Elections to the European Parliament* (Allen and Unwin, 1980).

conclusion to draw is that the EC is, or is moving towards, a political system which is sui generis, where traditional criteria can only be applied with caution. Nevertheless, this question is relevant to the discussion of transnational party co-operation as attention has re-focused in the 1970s on the potential and the deficiencies of the EC institutions and particularly on the European Parliament, whose enlarged powers are regarded afresh in the light of direct elections.

Secondly, the role of political parties in European integration has attracted new attention through impending direct elections as well as the progressive inclusion of new policy areas in the Community, giving it a more overtly political character. This leads to the arguments about the 'democratic deficit' in the EC, where the 'legislative' role is performed essentially not by the Parliament but the Council of Ministers, so that any serious influence of the political parties in the functioning of the Community has been indirect and transmitted through the policy decisions of their leaders in government who are usually subject to party pressures.

Thirdly, any examination of the potential of transnational party co-operation must touch on the elementary question of what is understood by a 'political party'. All member states are characterised by variations of party government, whereby competing parties provide the dominant channels of policy activity and political promotion and, indeed, the pluralism of political forces as the core feature of democracy is a vital prerequisite for Community membership—notably, with the post-dictatorship applications from Greece, Spain and Portugal. What is of interest here is that there are different versions of political parties within this democratic framework, and that this variation inevitably repeats itself in the European-level form of party activity.

Fourthly, there is the question of how transnational party co-operation dovetails with national party activity and whether it has much impact there. The unique development from the mid-1970s has been the fact that the three approaches to the party political element in European integration—the long-established European party groups, the positions of national parties on European policy and the newly emerging transnational (extra-parliamentary) organisational links—have begun to merge together after being somewhat separate or non-existent arenas for European party activity. The expectations concerning the party political consequences of direct elections have been clearly expressed by Douglas Hurd, British Conservative spokesman on European affairs:

> The European Parliament, like the Westminster Parliament, is organized on party lines, and the main responsibility for the relationship between the two will lie with the political parties. This is not to say that party discipline could be as strict in the European Parliament as it is at Westminster . . . but it is essential that they (the European MPs) and their staffs should be meshed into their political parties at home at all levels, from the leadership through the parliamentary party, the voluntary organizations, to the constituencies. Indeed, it will be in their own interests to keep this close connexion. They will rely upon it for their

election, for their constituency operations after the election, and for their re-election later. . . . Thus the immediate responsibility lies with the political parties . . . on the Continent as well as in Britain, the political parties must take the lead. They are now recruiting a new regiment of elected representatives to join their ranks. . . .[1]

The business of rectifying the 'democratic deficit' in the European Community is therefore no longer merely a vague desired aim, but also a functional necessity. New European-level party political pressures are emanating from the event of direct elections, so that it is viable to regard developments in the 1970s as representing an important new historical phase in transnational party co-operation. This short survey will consider in turn the three approaches to political parties and their involvement in transnational party co-operation.

---

[1]'Can the political parties rise to the European challenge?', article in *The Times,* 25 July, 1978.

II

The Euro-Parliamentary Dimension

Group activity at the Euro-Parliamentary level, with its history of more than 25 years, has illustrated all the facets of transnational party co-operation as defined in the previous chapter. The following questions therefore identify its main characteristics up to the time of direct elections. Firstly, to what extent have the institutional weaknesses of the European Parliament itself circumscribed the transnational development of the party groups? Secondly, what is their political and administrative importance within the Parliament? Thirdly, by what criteria can their activities be evaluated—are traditional ones relevant or do new ones have to be formulated? Finally, what impact could direct elections have on the future of this form of transnational activity?

The European Parliament

As observed earlier, transnational activity cannot be properly evaluated without reference to the institutional context in which it takes place. The European Parliament is primarily a scrutinising and consultative body, with advisory and supervisory powers over the legislative proposals produced by the Commission for approval by the Council of Ministers. It differs fundamentally from national parliaments (despite its name) in that it is not yet elected by universal suffrage. It is not a legislature—it does not formally initiate policy and its budgetary powers are minimal; the Community's executive is neither drawn from it nor responsible to it; it does not sit permanently; and it has no fixed location.

Group activity has inevitably lacked the immediate stimulus deriving from a governmental/opposition conflict, and suffered from the absence of the competition for political power and the lack of corresponding structure of rewards and penalties for performance in the political race. Nevertheless, during the 1970s it has gained some political impetus from small but significant increases in its budgetary powers; from enlargement which saw the arrival of the British Conservative delegation and the introduction of Westminster-style procedures; and in mid-1975 from the arrival of the British Labour delegation, comprising just under half anti-marketeers. As a consequence discussions have become more overtly political, while at the same time the content of Community policy interest has extended to include areas like external relations.

4

The political and administrative importance of the groups

The European Parliament comprises 198 members from 49 national parties, designated by 15 parliamentary assemblies or chambers in the nine Community countries, and they are divided into six political groupings:

Group	Number	Nationalities	Parties
Socialists	66	9	12
Christian Democrats	53	7	12
Liberals	23	8	14
European Conservatives	18	2	2
European Progressive Democrats	17	3	3
Communists	18	3	4
Independents	3	2	2

(as of October 1978)

This analysis of the importance of the groups identifies the organisational opportunities for the promotion of transnational activity in the Euro-Parliamentary sphere, and clarifies those factors which may inhibit or serve to weaken it.

Overall, the groups dominate the organisation of the Parliament. As the late Sir Peter Kirk, the Conservative group leader, expressed it in January 1973:

> One of the things I've discovered here this week is that this place is virtually run by five men—the leaders of the five main political groups. We must constantly decide how business should be handled.[1]

The groups nominate and elect the President of the Parliament and the 12 vice-Presidents, who with the President comprise the parliamentary bureau. This body, with the aid of the parliamentary secretariat and its secretary-general, directs all the activities of the Parliament and is responsible for liaison with Brussels. The bureau and the group chairmen form the 'enlarged bureau', which with the 12 standing committee chairmen (also appointed on a group basis) draws up the agenda of the plenary sessions. The much sought-after rapporteurships, which grant access to the administrative expertise of the Parliament's secretariat, are also the subject of group competition and allocation. In the debates, the group spokesmen are given priority and enjoy longer speaking time for the presentation of group viewpoints than do individual members, time being allotted according to group size. Permanent secretariats responsible for regular administration and co-ordination of the groups' activities are funded by the Parliament, the amount allocated being proportional to the size of each group and the number of nationalities contained in it. The *non-inscrits* (independent members) are subject to the major disadvantages of having less speaking time in debates, and not enjoying financial allowances for research assistance.

---

[1]Quoted in the *Observer,* 21 January, 1978.

Certain factors, however, act to modify this monopoly by the groups. The first is the committee system of the Parliament. Legislative proposals are channelled immediately into one of the 12 standing committees of the Parliament, so that the groups are excluded at this initial stage. The second is the appointment of committee rapporteurs on each issue arising in committee, which gives the individual Member of the European Parliament (MEP) extensive influence on the presentation of the final report to the plenary. The third is that these part time groups as a whole have relatively little opportunity to meet to discuss in depth the increasing number of proposals which the Parliament is being asked to consider.

Criteria applicable to this form of transnational activity

A necessary starting point in the analysis of transnational group activity is to determine the relevance of conventional criteria for examining parliamentary parties; for these may help to highlight the differences between this form of party activity and that at the national level, identifying any unique features.

The criteria traditionally applied to the analysis of parliamentary party groups at the national level can for analytical purposes be divided into 'external' and 'internal'. The 'external' criteria include: the government/opposition role; their historical development; and their policy orientation. The 'internal' criteria are: the nature of their leadership; the internal organisation; and their degree of cohesion and ideology. It may be said at the outset that the crucial and obvious difference between the party groups in the European Parliament and national parliamentary parties is that the former are not essentially involved in the power game, so that those political criteria associated with the winning of elections and the government/opposition roles are not applicable here. The remaining criteria will be applied in order to draw some conclusions on the nature of Euro-Parliamentary transnational activity.

The three largest groups—the Socialists, the Christian Democrats and the Liberals—were the founding groups of the ECSC Common Assembly in 1953, and so have the longest history of working transnationally in a European assembly. During the 1970s, the formation of the three smaller groups has contributed a broader party political dimension to the Parliament; the European Conservative group was formed on enlargement in January 1973, comprising British Conservatives, with a nominal Dane or two; the European Progressive Democrats, joining the Gaullists in a tactically motivated alliance with the Irish Fianna Fail members, was created in July 1973; while the Communist and Allies group was created in the autumn of that year when the French and the Italian Communists formed an official group. The groups therefore now represent the main political forces to be found in the Community countries. However, unlike parliamentary parties at the national level, their development has been somewhat artificially determined owing to the nature of appointment of MEPs by national parliaments. Also, because of the diffuse power structure of the European Community, the party groups cannot claim to have helped to guide the development of the 'political system' of which they potentially form a part.

Analysis of policy orientation at the national level assumes a commitment to or a concentration on the nation state. No similar assumption can clearly be made at the European level, so that any programmatic analysis of the party groups must not only include an examination of traditional beliefs which may be nationally orientated, but also their degree of commitment to European integration and the exact form that this should take.

National parliamentary parties usually outline their positions on all major issues in their manifestoes before general elections. They are theoretically committed to implementing as much of these as possible should they enter the next government. The discussion of the overall policy orientation of the party groups in the European Parliament is somewhat artificial, as the groups largely respond to the policy initiatives of the Commission and the Council of Ministers and, until the prospect of direct elections stimulated the formulation of common programmes for the party federations, the groups had nothing to resemble manifestoes. Some, however, had prepared ad hoc statements on certain aspects of Community policy in which they were particularly interested. The Socialist group, for example, adopted policy statements on the future of regional policy, on unemployment and on consumer policy, during 1977-78.

The applicable 'internal' features to be discussed are: the nature of the party group leadership; the characteristics of the internal organisation; and the degree of cohesion and ideology. The leader of a national parliamentary party is an actual or potential Prime Minister or senior minister. In the European party groups the leader is more first among equals, with no powers of patronage, and his role is primarily that of overcoming, incorporating and amalgamating the different interests or outlooks contained in each group. As at the national level, there are diverse ideological, policy and special interests, but these are further complicated in the Euro-parliamentary sphere by the inclusion of different nationals with their own specific demands and conditioned by their own languages and national restraints on their operation as MEPs.

Because of the role of the chairmen of the groups acting as brokers in the European Parliament, the internal organisation of a group is an important aid to the leader. In national politics, the leader and his frontbench team may meet regularly, individuals within the parliamentary party are in daily contact during sessions, and the whole body may have relatively frequent formal meetings. Because the European party groups are part-time, the leader must often make decisions on behalf of the absentee group without consulting it, and the organisation tends to be more regulated. The week prior to each plenary session is kept free of official parliamentary business for group meetings; they may meet for an hour each day before debates in the monthly week-long plenaries and the Parliament finances bi-annual study days. In the larger groups the working parties on policy contribute to the achievement of common policy positions, while the secretariats play an important part in this

7

political role of conciliation, arbitration and communication in an effort to reduce conflicts and reach a meaningful compromise. Despite these efforts, open disagreement may become apparent within group meetings and in debates when a group may appoint two 'official' spokesmen. In final votes, also, individuals may declare against their groups, or previously arranged voting agreements between different groups may break down.

As at the national level, cohesion is important in the Euro-Parliamentary groups but for different reasons. The unity of a national parliamentary party is considered a necessary prerequisite for establishing its credibility as a party of government or as an effective opposition. This problem does not apply at the Euro-Parliamentary level, but cohesion is nevertheless relevant for it strengthens the groups' claims to transnationality and it lends validity to the ideological traditions on which they are based.

Two major political factors contribute generally to the difficulties of achieving group unity: firstly, the number and diversity of the nationalities incorporated in the groups, and secondly, the range of ideological variations within the same political families. National differences predictably surface over support for European integration in general, and play a particularly important part where the home party is opposed to or reserved about the long term development of the Community. The most notable example is that of the Socialist group which had to relax its previously strict rules on internal group discipline in order to incorporate the sceptical Danes who joined on enlargement in 1973, and more so when the large British Labour delegation joined the group in 1975.

While the incorporation of many nationalities gives greater weight to a group's theoretical claim to transnationality, it places correspondingly more strains on the achievement of united, coherent and commonly agreed group policy positions, necessary to give political meaning to its transnational presence. Different nationals show a particular interest in specific Community policies, most notably the Germans in economic affairs and the French in agriculture. Conflicts may also arise between various nationals over different concerns—in the Socialist group, the Germans and the British often tend to pursue consumer interests while the French and the Irish support agricultural interests.

As in national party activity, a common ideological background and commitment to the same broad ideals does not automatically predetermine the ability of a party group to act as a united and coherent transnational body. Ideological disagreements similar to those present in national parliamentary parties are further complicated at the European level by the influence of different national political experiences, varied political cultures and diverse ideological inclinations. The Socialist group incorporates, for instance, streams of Socialist ideology which range from the near-Marxist to the reformist Social Democratic nearer the centre of the political spectrum. The Christian Democrats and the Liberals also incorporate a wide range of ideological interpretation, with the former including those who support a free market economy together with others who practise a statist approach to

8

economic affairs. Members of the Liberal group are regarded as ranging from progressive social reformers to diehard free traders.

From this discussion it can be seen that the organisational criteria which are employed in the analysis of parliamentary party activity at the national level are also applicable at the European level but in the context of the constitutional differences between the European Parliament and national parliaments political yardsticks can only be applied with basic qualifications.

The possible impact of direct elections

The immediate effect of direct elections will be that the European Parliament will become a permanent body, more than twice its existing size with 410 members given a mandate for five years. In the longer term there are four possibilities. One is to continue with the same relatively low profile, unlikely after the stimulus of direct elections and with a permanently constituted body of MEPs. Secondly, the European Parliament could work within the framework of its existing limited powers, but exploit them more fully. Thirdly, it could continue on the basis of these present powers, but demand modifications to give them more teeth, such as the right to dismiss individual Commissioners. Or, fourthly, the Parliament could demand outright greater powers such as the initiation of a broader range of legislation.

Only the second and third of these possibilities are considered the most likely in the short and medium term; this is because, despite the political potential offered to the European Parliament by direct elections its fundamental constitutional weaknesses cannot be erased easily as this would involve discussion of the overall structure of the Community, whereby any changes are conditional on the unanimous consent of the member-states. The groups cannot therefore commit themselves to implementing the programmes of the party federations. In the short term, the Parliament will probably continue to have a nomadic existence based on the three centres of Luxembourg, Strasbourg and Brussels. A low electoral turnout, furthermore, would weaken its claim to represent the electorates of the Community and devalue its claim to an enhanced legislative role.

It is projected that after direct elections the relative strengths of the groups will remain the same, with the Communists possibly replacing the Liberals as the third largest group. Such projections, however, assume many constants: that there are no major national voting upheavals; that voting patterns at the national level will apply in the European sphere; that group alignments remain the same; that the qualifications for forming a group remain basically unchanged; and that no new political groupings emerge in the Parliament elected in 1979.

Undoubtedly, the relatively full time nature of the groups will increase their socialising effects. This could well lead to an increased group identification and a corresponding increase in group loyalty, so facilitating the achievement of a common group viewpoint and promoting group cohesion. Despite this prospect, the multifarious national outlooks and ideological complexities will basically continue to make group unity difficult to achieve, and inevitably the linguistic barriers will continue as a problematical hurdle to uninhibited internal communication. The ultimate impact of direct elections on transnational party activity will consequently depend on three categories of factors: those associated with the campaign and its effects; the nature and composition of the new body of MEPs; and the development of institutional relationships within the Community.

The issues raised in the campaign and the extent to which they are European, national or local, and how much they are pursued by individuals in the newly constituted groups, may help to determine the orientation and impetus of the newly elected Parliament. These issues may affect media coverage and accordingly the maintenance of interest in the Parliament after the excitement of the election has abated. The level of turnout in the campaign will affect the status of the Parliament, the higher it is the greater the importance of the Parliament as a representative institution.

The second group of factors relate to the new body of MEPs: notably, the criteria by which candidates are chosen in their respective countries; their previous political experience, depth of commitment to Europe and their own personalities, political motives, linguistic ability and particular interests. The question must also be raised as to whom MEPs become responsible—would it be their group, their European party organisation, their national party links or local interests. The role which they and the new groups seek for themselves both within the Parliament and in the Community would also be important factors.

Finally, of crucial importance is the attitude to the newly elected Parliament of the other Community institutions and of the national parliaments; the institutional relationships and systems of accountability established after direct elections; and the as yet unformulated triangular relationship between the party groups, the party federations, and the national parties.

Despite these various reservations and factors conditioning the future development of the European Parliament, it may be said with little hesitation that direct elections ought to witness a new historical departure for Euro-Parliamentary party activity involving a qualitative change in the status and functioning of the transnational groups.

III

The Transnational Party Organisational Dimension

From the mid-1970s there have developed various transnational party organisations, which are both restricted to the member states of the Community and geared to some basic form of European-level party activity: the Confederation of Socialist Parties of the European Community was formed in 1974, followed by the Federation of Liberal and Democratic Parties of the European Community (ELD) and the (Christian Democratic) European People's Party (EPP), both in 1976. These are the three prime examples, although the new habit of European organisational co-ordination has also spread to smaller party groupings, including regional nationalists, the extreme right and even the ecologists. The main exception to this recent trend has been the Communists, who have refused to engage in what they regard as an 'electioneering' exercise.

The exact potential and political importance of these European party federations is unclear at this relatively early stage. As a less established feature of the transnational party scene than the party groups in the European Parliament, their recent and somewhat hesitant formation provokes several basic doubts. Are they more than convenient arrangements or loose umbrella associations for the purpose of providing a 'European' colouring to the activities of a multiplicity of national parties in the direct elections campaign? Do they have any essential or necessary functions, even in a minimal sense? To what extent may they together with the European Parliament groups be considered as embryonic European political parties in any traditional sense? To emphasise the novelty of the European party federations is to discount the older party political Internationals—the Socialist International reformed after the Second World War in 1951, the Liberal International formed in 1947 and the European Christian Democratic Union (UEDC) in 1965 as the successor of the Nouvelles Equipes Internationales (NEI) established in 1947. Since these have been no more than purely consultative and have not confined their deliberations to EC matters, they cannot be regarded as integrationist as the European party federations intend to be in some form or other.

The term 'federation' as applied to the new European party formations is, of course, misleading although for practical purposes useful, not only because each one has adopted a different nomenclature but also because, strictly, it refers to their future possibilities rather than to their present state.

Clearly, the party federations may be dismissed as of now as essentially peripheral as political factors—they are brand new, without any specific tradition or precedent to strengthen their claims, apart from a general affiliation to a recognised ideological stream, and furthermore they cannot avoid the reality that the national focus of activity continues to claim prior if not overriding attention in the thinking of individual political parties. Nevertheless, they are probably one of the best measures of the (European) politicising effect of direct elections in 1979 even though high expectations of this first round of European voting are unrealistic. Whatever the individual reasons offered for the formation of the federations—e.g., the absence of a party organisational framework to complement the party groups, the example set by European-level pressure and interest group associations, the desire to promote democratic legitimation in the EC—it is undeniable that forthcoming direct elections (a realistic prospect since 1974) have forced their development. Accordingly, the experience of these first European elections can only assist further this process towards transnational party organisations, though in what precise manner remains to be seen. In short, the growth of the federations at the same time as the move towards the deadline of the elections is hardly coincidental. In addition, both events have proceeded against the background of the enlarging scope of EC policy activity (e.g. in the external relations field). All these factors point to an increased political presence for the Community as a whole, though this says little automatically about its internal cohesion or the nature of its institutional structure.

Even in their so far brief history, the federations have been the subject of varying interpretations, congregating around two schools of thought: that the federations are essentially very loose structures with primarily an electoral purpose and little real prospect for cohesive activity beyond that; and that in spite of their obvious limitations these new formations are incipient federal bodies whose potential must not be rejected. There is some room for overlap between these two interpretations, notably in the inclination of both to refer to the US model of a party system which can on the one hand be taken as loose and on the other as working within a federal structure. It is nevertheless the view of the authors that the American model of party development is not really appropriate as a point of departure for analysing transnational party co-operation in the European Community, since this activity can only be measured by the criteria of European party development of which the constituent parties are themselves prime examples.[1]

It is also relevant to consider on a more specific basis how much features and problems evident over time in the operation of the long-established European parliamentary groups have begun to repeat themselves with the party federations, such as the diversity of policy attitudes within ideological tendencies and the imprint of national outlooks on the European positions of

---

[1] See Geoffrey Pridham and Pippa Pridham, 'The New European Party Federations and Direct Elections in *The World Today,* February 1979, esp. pp. 64-65.

individual parties.[2] Also, the party federations may reflect different kinds of party relationships as in European party development itself. For instance, Christian Democrats have tended to espouse looser party formations compared with European Socialists, who invariably have adopted more readily bureaucratic norms in the elaboration of their national party structures. Equally, the former have accorded a greater value than the latter to European federalism as a central tenet of their ideological outlook since the very initiation of Christian Democratic parties after the Second World War. Such broad differences are bound to influence the approaches of these respective forces towards European transnational party co-operation. Whereas the statutes of the Christian Democratic European People's Party emphasise 'close and permanent collaboration' between its member parties 'in order to implement their common policy in the construction of a federal Europe' (article 3), the first president of the Socialist Confederation, Wilhelm Dröscher, reflected the weight of national party structural traditions when he observed:

> It must be quite clearly noted that the development of a 'European Socialist Party' is not a realistic possibility in the near future. This would create insoluble problems for the national parties. But it is essential that in this transition stage the member parties of the Confederation should be united in a 'family of parties', which . . . sees to it that the policy of democratic socialism does not remain a dead letter in the European Community.[3]

Given that no integrated or detailed analysis of the European party federations comparable to that of national party systems or individual national parties is yet possible in such an early stage of their development, what is attempted here is a construction of their specific relevant features along the lines of European party comparative analysis. The following points relate to the general questions posed at the start of this section of the survey, although any conclusions can be no more than tentative.

The constitutional basis of the federations and their institutional interlinkage within the European Community
The three federations have already formulated basic structural requirements, as their statutes indicate. These provisions offer some constitutional basis for their further evolution as conventional 'parties'. For instance, they include in each case a president, vice-presidents, an executive organ, a small secretariat and a congress. Such transnational arrangements are inevitably more cumbersome than their equivalents at the national level. As Florus Wijsenbeek, secretary-general of the Liberal Federation, has noted, 'these

---

[2]See Stanley Henig (ed), *Political Parties in the European Community,* chapter 12, p. 279 and passim.
[3]Quoted in full in Stanley Henig, op. cit., p. 285.

congresses are somewhat difficult to convene—they require long and careful preparation, particularly because of the number of languages involved, and it is thus more difficult for them to fulfil the watchdog or brains trust function carried out by national party congresses'.

More interest dwells on the functions or powers of these various bodies as a portent of possible future developments. Here the very limited scope for their activity as outlined in the respective statutes is hardly surprising. The least potentially 'federal' of the three is predictably the Socialist one, which reflects the strong emphasis on the autonomy of its member parties in the provision that its congress may take binding decisions on a two-thirds majority but only after a unanimous recommendation by its bureau (consisting primarily of national party representatives). With the Christian Democratic EPP, the political bureau has relatively wide powers for it may take decisions by majority, although its statutes similarly recognise that member parties 'shall retain their name, their identity and their freedom of action within the framework of their national responsibilities' (article 2).

On the wider question of the federations' place or potential status in the institutional structure of the European Community, there are some pointers but clearly the broader problem of their overall political role is an open matter depending on any structural reforms which might strengthen the 'supranational' institutions. Two aspects are however worth mentioning. Firstly, the question of the federations' relationship with their respective party groups in the European Parliament is an obvious one in following the conventional approach of European party analysis. Already links have been established both constitutionally and in practice. The participation of the group leadership in the executive organ of the federation is provided for by the statutes in each case, while the Liberal Federation has gone furthest in permitting its congress to receive reports from the group and make recommendations to it (article 26). At the bureaucratic level, the link has been underlined in the case of the Christian Democrats, where the secretary-general of the group also performs as the secretary-general of the EPP, while common to all three federations is the interchange or sharing of some staff between their secretariats and administrative personnel from the groups. Certainly until direct elections both groups and federations have a firm common cause in furthering the very activity of transnational party co-operation, although it is to be expected that in the intermediate future, with possibly increased political weight of the European Parliament, differences must emerge between the groups and federations if only because of their distinct roles as parliamentary and organisational factors. At this stage, it is unclear how much political blood will flow eventually through these constitutional arteries.

Secondly, a faint link is already visible between the federations and the European Commissioners as representing that 'supranational' institution with some executive functions. All three statutes acknowledge the party political affiliation of Commissioners through their inclusion as members of the executive organs. However, this tenuous relationship can be reckoned as no more than symbolic at this point of development with regard to a possible

14

relationship between a European executive and potential legislature.

One further undeveloped feature to be watched is whether or how European-level interest groups such as trade unions and agricultural associations will relate to these incipient party federations. In essence, that will proceed from the impression created by the federations during direct elections and after, and whether they acquire any legitimation as channels of political activity. So far these interest groups have only begun to take note of the European Parliament where this has some influence on decision making.[4] Finally, the lesson should be drawn from European party development that informal procedures count strongly in how party formations evolve and shape themselves: 'The organisation of parties depends essentially on unwritten practice and habit . . . constitutions and rules never give more than a partial idea of what happens'.[5] A major qualification has to be made here which is that this whole exercise of transnational party co-operation is complicated by the often spasmodic interlinkage between European-level and national institutional arrangements, and that the 'jealous' autonomy of national member parties must make constitutional rules or the effort to establish them all the more vital in the operation of the party federations.

The envisaged electoral role of the federations and patterns of their political activity

Two questions are pertinent here: will the federations be largely responsible for providing the European dimension for direct elections, which would otherwise be simply a collection of co-terminous national campaigns, and as such will they enter party political dialogue? What permanent political features are in the offing in that the federations may already be developing functions which cast ahead beyond the event of direct elections? The answer to both questions should provide some clue to the further political role of the European party federations.

The first question is by way of asking how necessary the federations will be in the direct elections campaign. The precise role of the federations is still in a formative stage as of the moment of writing, but it is generally understood they will contribute some 'commercial' ingredient with the production of common posters and stickers as well as their assistance in formulating common slogans and facilitating the exchange of speakers between member countries. A more serious purpose will be sufficient co-ordination between the various parties belonging to a federation to prevent the occurrence of glaring discrepancies in the enunciation of electoral aims or the pursuance of polemical arguments. On the other hand, flexibility will invariably be recognised in the conduct of national party campaigns. This has been stated, in principle, by Robert Pontillon, second president of the Socialist Confederation, when he remarked following its agreement on a political

---

[4]John Fitzmaurice, *The European Parliament,* Saxon House (1978), p. 93.
[5]Maurice Duverger. *Political Parties.* Methuen (1964). p. xvi.

declaration in June 1978 that 'the points of accord between our parties, the general principles, are binding for all', and that each member party would take up themes in the declaration and define them according to each national political situation.

Here there is a point of convergence between the three federations, which are distinguished by their integrative potential, and other European electorally-motivated party formations. The principal one among the latter is the European Democratic Union (EDU), an alliance of Conservative and some Christian Democratic parties in Western Europe (including some from outside the EC). Although this might acquire permanent political functions as yet unclear, its overriding purpose was originally very much electoral—in particular, to provide a European organisational framework for the campaign of certain member parties, above all the British Conservatives, who for ideological reasons have remained outside the established federations. Evidently, a sense of organisational competition has helped to promote this development. The contrasting example is offered by the French and Italian Communists who although members of the same party group in the European Parliament have rejected any idea of an equivalent organisational formation for direct elections. The reasons lie partly in the ideological ambiguities of 'Eurocommunism' (which in their view cannot be expressed in any structural form), and also in a basic reluctance to adopt what appears to them merely as a convenient electoral arrangement—in view of the fact that Communists generally prefer to justify their activity in ideological terms.

While European-level party organisation has 'arrived' in the preliminary period before direct elections, an examination of the second question suggests that the three federations at least are looking beyond this event in the delineation of their activities. Does this then imply that they are on the way to becoming future European political parties? In such a process basic difficulties would arise all along the line, one of which undoubtedly is programmatic. Already the relatively modest construction of federation programmes for the elections has provided some foretaste of such problems of homogeneity between national parties (this will be discussed in Chapter IV).

There are other signs that the federations are planning for a long term future. Firstly, they see themselves as having a continuing and permanent role to play. This is apparent from their official statements, speeches of their leading figures and even from their statutes. The Liberal Federation, for example, views direct elections as only one of its three aims, the others being the formulation of a common position on EC matters in general and the involvement of the public 'in the construction of a united and liberal Europe' (article 2). Secondly, the question of political alliances at the European level has been voiced with the implication this has for the post-electoral balance of political forces in the European Parliament. This thought has been most pointedly stated on the centre-right, where interest has focused on the possibility of some arrangement between Christian Democrats and Conservatives. The motivation, which owes much to anti-'Marxism', was powerfully evident in the establishment of the EDU in April 1978. On the European left, the question of alliances is inextricable from the thorny problem of the relations between Socialists and Communists, which has a history much older than that of the European Community itself, so that discussion of this matter has been in very muted terms. Thirdly, the element of long term strategy in the thinking of the federations is underlined by the contacts they have fostered with their fraternal parties from the applicant countries Greece, Spain and Portugal. This has taken the form of bilateral assistance (financial and moral) from member parties of the federations, and mutual visits between officials of the federations and leaders of the national parties concerned. A strong reason for this activity is to prepare for their future inclusion in both the federations and the party groups, and hence reinforce party solidarity within an enlarged Community and assure the future balance of European political forces there.

In conclusion, it may be pointed out that the electoral motivation or orientation of the European party federations should not be underrated as a political function, for fighting election campaigns is a central purpose of political parties in a democratic framework, and in many cases is their primary purpose. In this sense, the prospect of direct elections has been crucial in the development of the federations, just as the prospect of regular European elections in the future will guarantee them a permanent role. They are therefore a serious proposition in the future evolution of the Community, though their actual potential is far from certain and it is necessary not to be too optimistic about their future political impact. Their importance is hedged with many reservations, the most decisive of which is the national focus of party-political activity, which will now be considered.

IV

The National Party Frameworks and Transnational Co-operation

The national level of activity continues to claim prior if not overriding attention in the thinking of individual political parties, which consequently places a fundamental limitation on their willingness to merge their sovereignty within the framework of party co-operation at the European level. This is to state a truism, and one of course in line with the broad contours of European integration development in the 1970s towards 'inter-governmental' arrangements (though, it must be emphasised, within the EC frame of reference). In order, however, to establish this approach on an analytical plane, it is necessary to focus on specific ways in which the transnational co-operation is conditioned by national political considerations. These would include the nature and intensity of links between member parties and federations, how much the former take the latter seriously and for what reasons and whether these EC-wide organisational relationships have created new pressures in the operation of national parties despite the general emphasis on their autonomy. At the same time, it is important to examine those wider factors deriving from the national political forum which promote or impede transnational party co-operation.

What essentially is being considered here is the vertical as distinct from the horizontal dimension of transnational party co-operation—that is, the impact of national party outlooks not to mention differences within them on European-level activity. It must be remembered that the vast proportion of those involved in the working of the federations are national party 'actors' (wearing maybe their European hats, though in many cases circumspectly) aside from such European 'actors' as party group leaders (themselves also national MPs), European Commissioners (who play here only a formal role) and party Eurocrats (whose purpose is administrative, not political). In short, the activities of the federations are channelled vertically through the national party structures; indeed, exclusively so, since the federations have no vertical structures and consultation procedures. It seems appropriate, therefore, to consider three points of focus in discussing both the inter-relationship of national member parties with the federations and those general promotive or restraining factors which condition this process from the national angle: the party-traditional, the political-functional and the socio-political.

The party-traditional factor
This covers such questions as the influence of individual party traditions (e.g., of an internationalist kind) and whether these encourage a positive or negative attitude towards the European Community in general and transnational co-operation in particular, and most notably the imprint of party ideology on Europe. The hypothesis here is that there is a strong interlinkage of an individual party's positions on different EC issues, whether these include the very principle of European integration, areas of common policy, direct elections, or the powers of the European Parliament and that this strongly colours its approaches to party co-operation. Clearly, a national political party which is a priori favourable towards the progress of the EC and inspired by the political significance of direct elections is likely to be predisposed to espouse transnational activity. In looking at these questions it is relevant to bear in mind the erosion of the traditional distinction between foreign and domestic issues in national politics, a problem often raised in the context of European integration in the 1970s but also applicable to the subject of party political harmonisation.

There are a variety of ways of estimating the impact of party traditions on transnational party co-operation. Two would include the extent to which individual parties may accord a high priority to European policy positions, and whether the concept of national sovereignty is present as an element within a given party's ideological outlook. It is to be expected that the two features are mutually exclusive, seeing that a negative European stand is unlikely to be expressed in the form of a composite scheme for European integration. Few national parties have elaborated European programmes as such—discounting those which have been issued by parties especially for direct elections (for example the German Social Democratic Party (SPD) in September 1978, with many others to follow). The Giscardian Independent Republicans outlined a 'programme for Europe' in October 1966, and in 1972, the West German CDU presented an 'action programme' on Europe. Of course, this must not be a compelling index of attachment to European ideals; the prize for ideologically motivated support for European positions must be awarded to the Christian Democrats—the post-war French Mouvement Républicain Populaire (MRP) (since disbanded among various parties of the same tendency),[1] the CDU which has retained Adenauer's emphatic backing for West Germany's 'European' vocation (and has been called by its leader Helmut Kohl 'the classical party of European Integration') as well as the Italian Democrazia Cristiana (DC) and Tindemans' Social Christians in Belgium. It is accurate to say that with the Christian Democratic parties, European integration has been accepted as part of their ideological traditions, founded as these parties were in

---

[1] See Henig, op. cit., pp. 74-5.

the aftermath of the second World War when nationalistic values had been discredited by the Fascist experience.

The opposite ideological pole of national sovereignty provides a further guide in a negative way to a party's willingness to become involved in transnational activity. The two extreme examples are the French Gaullists and the British Labour Party, both of which underline the connection between a pronounced ideological outlook on European integration and a specific stand on direct elections and transnational co-operation. It is valid here to question whether it is possible to refer to party tradition in a simple fashion, for this may be either ideological or assume vaguer forms like a party's 'belief system' or its 'way of life'. Furthermore, ideological assumptions over Europe may be the subject of internal party divisions (notably with the British Labour Party, and to some lesser extent the French Socialists), which leads one to ask how much transnational co-operation linked to pro/anti-European outlooks permeates downwards to the activist level.

The concept of national sovereignty has in the context of direct elections been stated probably in its purest form by Michel Debré, leader of the traditional wing of the Gaullists, whose assertions about France's 'independence' as being threatened by an upgraded European Parliament bear a remarkable similarity to his anti-integration speeches as de Gaulle's prime minister in the early 1960s. Undoubtedly, these traditionalist pressures have influenced the confusing tactics of the Chirac-led Rassemblement pour la République (RPR) over direct elections. Sometimes ideological stands assume an indirect or tactical character as, for instance, in the concentration of Debré on attacking the specific voting system to be adopted for European elections. Similarly, the link between ideological positions on Europe and the future role of the European Parliament were illustrated vividly when at the British Labour Party conference of September 1976 the principle of direct elections was rejected decisively. The 'anti'-position was explained by Ian Mikardo, who argued that direct elections would 'move Europe on from being an economic community to becoming a single, entrenched, capitalist superstructure', not to mention that in his view they would produce an electoral 'massacre' for Labour.

It goes without saying that Labour reservations about involvement in the Socialist Confederation reflect a *leitmotiv* in the party's attitude on Europe throughout the postwar period, despite the support of some of its government leaders for British entry to the EEC in the later 1960s. A dominant theme in this attitude has been a determination to oppose the loss of national control over economic and monetary policy making (e.g., see the Labour election manifestoes of 1974, as well as the party's negative stand on the issue of the European Monetary System (EMS) in 1978 which was consistent with its negative attitude towards direct elections). The British Labour Party has been exceptional in the extent to which European issues have become deeply embedded in traditional left/right divisions within itself, a feature repeated only in the Danish case among other Socialist parties in the Community; although it should be noted that in its principled concern for party autonomy the British party is really an extreme version of a common phenomenon present among its fraternal parties on the Continent.

Both these major considerations—the priority given to European issues, and the concern for national sovereignty and autonomy—have entered and profoundly affected the discussion of programmes for the European party federations. This has been most pointedly evident in the Socialist Confederation, where the British Labour Party's hostility to any ripple of federalist sympathies in the draft programme occasioned its opposition to further progress in producing a final version. Such contention is not so surprising among Socialist parties, who more than other political forces have traditionally exhibited a habit of relatively open programmatic debate, witnessed in the insistence of parties other than Labour on the inclusion of specific national policy interests in the programme (e.g., co-determination) not always to the liking of their partners in the confederation.

With the other two federations, such problems have been more muted although similar problems have arisen. This is partly because, as with the Christian Democrats, there has been a strong reliance on pragmatism and hence flexibility of policy outlook coupled with pronounced European convictions. Although both factors reduced controversy over the EPP's European programme, differences nevertheless emerged with an ideological flavour over such matters as social policy and economic planning even if traditions of party solidarity meant these were voiced less publicly. In the case of the Liberals, party 'patriotism' has been less pronounced; the Liberals are smaller political forces in their respective countries, so that the process of European programmatic formulation has been relatively easy though not without some friction (e.g. over the preamble) and, indeed, the Liberals were the first to publish a finalised programme (in late 1977). Even so, high expectations were not attached to this exercise for as Wijsenbeek, the ELD secretary-general, commented: 'the platforms drawn up by these federations as yet tend to . . . sound out one another's ideas rather than trace out political guidelines actually to be followed'. Internal party involvement in the detailed formulation of European programmes has been very largely the preserve of European specialists although local activist elements have in some cases (notably the Socialists) been fully aware of these deliberations.

There are various other pointers to the impact of party traditions on trans-national co-operation. Three in particular deserve brief attention. The question of federation membership itself has in a few instances brought to the surface conflicts of party identity, especially among the Liberals who more than the other two comprise a very mixed political grouping, e.g. the objections from within the British party over the inclusion of the Giscardian Republicans in the ELD, and the consequent withdrawal from membership of the French Radicals. Closer association with parties of the same ideological school, which however espouse divergent paths of identity, has in its own way exacerbated points of tension, often in relation to specific issues (e.g., the criticisms by the Dutch Labour Party of the SPD policy on the controversial Berufsverbot). Secondly, the status of European 'actors' *(Europapolitiker)* within their own national parties must offer some clues about individual parties' orientation towards the EC, although this cannot avoid the general trend (at least in the whole period up to direct elections) whereby members of the European Parliament and others involved in transnational co-operation have enjoyed little more than a peripheral role on the domestic front. The main exception is the Netherlands where, for example, the first Den Uyl government from 1973 contained as many as eight former MEPs. Finally, traditions of party internationalism play an inevitable part in the readiness to engage in transnational co-operation. Here, habits of mind have passed from the various Internationals, where for example the German SPD has followed an active role in both the Socialist International (of which its chairman Willy Brandt has been president since November 1976) and the Socialist Confederation. Conversely, the British Labour Party's traditional preference for looser party 'bridge-building' than more integrated activities clearly throws much light on its attitude towards the aims of the Socialist Confederation. This contrasts somewhat with its rival the British Conservatives, who in line with their conventional support for European links have been developing spontaneously branch 'twinning' arrangements with local associations of the West German CDU.

In short, these various 'leads' do underline how much traditional party positions on European integration in general do provide the essential matrix from which their involvement in transnational co-operation is formed. Of course, party positions on Europe may over time be modified, such as by the dictates of governmental responsibility, although much depends on the degree of party identity and the direction of ideological motivation of a particular national party.

The political-functional factor
The same method of analysis will be adopted here, namely defining several pointers to the inter-relationship between national parties and transnational co-operation and drawing qualified conclusions. One or two general observations are however relevant to the ensuing discussion. The criticism that certain political parties, which are pro-European (especially Socialist ones) but have failed to transmit their convictions into policy action at home, is valid in a sense but also one sided in that it ignores the many domestic political constraints on most areas of policy making. Admittedly, foreign policy has been less subject to these, but it is worth emphasising again that European integration cannot be classified as conventional external politics, if only because of the strong overlap of EC policy concerns into the domestic arena. Political parties have not failed to accept the full implications of this distinction, whether or not they have been pro-integrationist in outlook. In addition, it is already apparent in the combined context of transnational party development and the process towards direct elections since 1974 that European considerations have more than ever before entered the calculations of party leaders in multifarious ways. With this it is possible to speak of a growing European dimension, though it need not necessarily amount always to a

'Europeanisation' of national party politics. Insofar as European integration has come to involve, in practice, the dovetailing between national and *communautaire* positions, it is legitimate with regard to the harmonisation of party activities to focus also on the 'internalisation' of European questions. In other words, this is a two-way process.

One salient political-functional feature must be the question of the primacy of national politics in terms of expenditure and pressures of time, the demands of everyday politics especially with parties in office and, above all, the fact that the power struggle is set in the national context. All these constraints inevitably impose short-term perspectives, while the transnational exercise requires some attention to the intermediate if not long-term approach. All the same, the deadline of direct elections has itself created new pressures and helped to close the gap somewhat between these two approaches. Helmut Schmidt, who as Chancellor has presided over a trend in West German European policy towards more overtly national positions, has commented on the forthcoming European campaign as 'a kind of prior decision for our own national elections'. It is also predictable that opposition politicians in particular should be interested in the European stage as an alternative opportunity for public exposure, though clearly this attraction must be limited by the extent to which European activity receives coverage at home. At the British Conserverative party conference in October 1978, Douglas Hurd, while acknowledging that the approaching national election would be given priority, asserted that European elections would 'have to engage the energies of the whole party'. As if not to be caught unprepared by his party's rival, Labour's general secretary, Ron Hayward, emphasised the need for the party to commit itself to fighting direct elections so as not to 'hand victory on a plate to the Tories'. Evidently, there is a tendency for party organisers to believe that 'elections are elections' so that the spirit of competition even arises when political power is not directly involved as with the European campaign, i.e., it is domestically motivated because the latter also reflects on the state of the respective parties. This consideration is clearly operative with smaller parties, who although their prospects for seats in the European Parliament might be modest or non-existent nevertheless show every sign of wanting to defend their particular interests, e.g., the Scottish National Party's determination to fight for 'Scottish representation' in Europe; the efforts by the Italian neo-Fascist Movimento Sociale Italiano (MSI) leader to recoup his party's chances and his own fading political career through an intensive tour of European capitals to re-activate contacts with other groups on the extreme right.

A further pointer to the influence of national political functions on transnational co-operation is the problem of domestic political alliances, specifically parties in coalition government with each other although this may also apply to parties which form opposition or electoral alliances (e.g., the Parti Communiste Français (PCF) and Parti Socialiste (PS) in France, 1972-77). By their very nature such relationships tend to be ambiguous even in the national context, so it is to be expected that such ambiguity must overflow into the parties' European activities. Transnational organisational links can of course both intensify and exacerbate internal alliances, depending on the current circumstances of the national political situations. The diverse domestic approaches of Socialist parties vis-à-vis their compatriotic Communist parties have caused unmanageable problems of co-ordination within the Confederation with the de facto acceptance of the principle of agreeing to disagree; similarly, wide differences among members of the European People's Party exist over the move towards the 'historic compromise' in Italy producing an unbridgeable gulf, in particular between the DC left and the Bavarian Christlich-Soziale Union (CSU). The issue at stake behind such problems is that of the 'right of intervention' between parties in the same European party organisation, an issue which has remained largely unspoken because it is too provocative at this early stage of transnational co-operation.

Finally, the political-functional factor cannot be viewed without mention of the power structure within national parties. This point would include the extent to which European policy making is the exclusive right of key national leaders (e.g., Marchais's sudden reversal of the PCF's position on direct elections, April 1977) or open to wider consultation within the party; whether European positions and hence transnational links become involved with the internal balance of power, and if this is unstable whether European positions are primarily motivated by the need to buttress the leadership; and of course the impact of government versus opposition roles via the consequently modified party power structure on European positions. It is fairly obvious that individual parties' approaches to transnational co-operation must at different times be affected by such considerations.

These various influences and pressures grouped together in this discussion of the political-functional factor all incline to show that on examination the assumption about the national focus of political activity does not necessarily prove that all the weight of party-political considerations are in one direction. In the wake of direct elections transnational party activity has already begun to acquire a new seriousness.

The socio-political factor
This factor is really shorthand for a variety of different influences emanating from the national political environment which can be summarised briefly. Firstly, there is the public-political dimension. The degree of politicisation over EC issues and the likely impression of direct elections on the various Community audiences are both determined by the extent to which the public in each country is interested as such in 'Europe' and favourably conditioned by Community activity. Mass media treatment of direct elections and transnational activity will be vital, but all the same the parties concerned will be operating against the background of divergent trends of public outlook towards the EC between member states, as the regular Euro-barometer surveys conducted under the auspices of the European Commission demonstrate. Ultimately, each national party is answerable to its own electorate back home whether this be in the setting of a national or European campaign. Furthermore, one may note that parties across Europe of the same ideological

tendency do not necessarily face the same type of voting groups, e.g. the Irish Labour Party works within a largely rural environment unlike Socialist parties elsewhere; Belgian Social Christians have strong trade union links unlike say German Christian Democrats. In other words, each national electorate is differently structured socially and within that framework party-political electoral constellations must vary.

Secondly, the domestic position of political parties may be profoundly affected by structural changes in their own party systems deriving from long-term socio-political developments. During the 1970s the party systems of seven of the nine member countries of the Community have undergone some structural change, the two exceptions being the Federal Republic and Ireland.[2]

In Denmark and Belgium the electoral rise of previously fringe or of new parties has been remarkable, in the latter case with the persistent dominance through this decade of the linguistic community problem and the new prominence of Flemish and Francophone sectional parties. Any reduction or increase in the electoral fortunes of the larger parties may influence the weight carried by such parties in European activity and, indeed, their ability to concentrate on the European elections themselves because of new domestic preoccupations.

Thirdly, there are a variety of influences which may be termed 'political-cultural'. These would include above all national outlooks towards other member countries of the Community which have sometimes coloured the way EC policy objectives are received by domestic audiences. These may be historically conditioned or culturally motivated, e.g. anti-German sentiments which remain a generation after the Second World War, French pride in the national language. It is conceivable that such attitudes may arise during the course of the European campaign, as all elections intensify political feelings, for they have not remained absent from the activities of the party federations.

It is evident from this survey of the three approaches to the party political element in European integration—the Euro-Parliamentary dimension, the transnational party-organisational dimension and the importance of national party frameworks—that a significant transformation has been ushered in in the area of European party co-operation. It must be reckoned that this process will continue, although the potential of this re-activation of transnational activity remains subject to the multiplicity of factors examined in this short study. In the first case, the longer established form of parliamentary transnational co-operation will undoubtedly undergo some fundamental change by virtue of the fact that future MEPs will enjoy the legitimacy of electoral approval. The growth of Community-wide party organisational relationships has because of its very novelty an even less determinable future as much will depend on the extent to which the federations will capitalise on the mobilisation occasioned by direct elections. Meanwhile, the national angle of transnational party co-operation in the context of developments since 1974

---

[2]Henig, op. cit., p. 300.

underlines that the hitherto largely separate theatres of national and European party activity have commenced a slow and laborious process of rapprochement. Accordingly, it may be said that, whether the motive of individual parties in seeking a transnational relationship is cosmetic dovetailing for electoral purposes or programmatic harmonisation for the sake of shaping the future course of the European Community along more political lines, this exercise has many interesting possibilities.

European Centre for Political Studies
European Cultural Foundation

Political Parties in the European Community

edited by
Stanley Henig

Contents

1 Introduction STANLEY HENIG

2 Belgium XAVIER MABILLE and VAL R. LORWIN

3 Denmark JOHN FITZMAURICE

4 France MICHAEL STEED

5 The Federal Republic of Germany TONY BURKETT

6 Ireland B. CHUBB

7 Italy P. A. ALLUM

8 Luxembourg MARIO HIRSCH

9 The Netherlands HANS DAALDER

10 The United Kingdom STANLEY HENIG

11 Transnational Parties in the European Community I:
The Party Groups in the European Parliament
GEOFREY PRIDHAM and PIPPA PRIDHAM

12 Transnational Parties in the European Community II:
The Development of European Party Federations
GEOFREY PRIDHAM and PIPPA PRIDHAM

13 Conclusion STANLEY HENIG

GEORGE ALLEN & UNWIN
POLICY STUDIES INSTITUTE

George Allen & Unwin. £10.50 hardback, £4.95 paperback